# Dedicated to:

*My beloved late mother, who stood in solidarity with the Black community by way of the public school system. Her hard work, passion, and dedication was the definition of solidarity with our most vulnerable and innocent.*

*The over 750 officers and countless peaceful citizens, including precious and innocent children, that have been made to feel afraid, were injured, killed, and had their livelihoods destroyed by the reckless behavior of anarchists.*
*Those who know truth see you.*
*We hear you.*
*We care.*

**Diet Woke Leftists/Progressives.**
**Members of KLANtifa.**
**Their supporters.**
**Their funders.**
**Their sympathizers.**
(Don't worry, it's an easy read. There are already flames on it so you don't have to burn it. You can do this!)

# Preface

I am not here to comfort you. I am here to AWAKEN you.
(rudely? Maybe.)

Do not fear

Keep your mind OPEN

**DO NOT COMPLY**
**with the agenda or concept of self-hatred.**

The following excerpts are simply
food for thought.
These words will provoke emotion, often heavy.

THINK CRITICALLY about them throughout each day

Use your plethora of lived
experience and your
*beautiful heart*
to draw <u>**logical conclusions**</u>

*MEDITATE* on these concepts, questions, and

their answers.

Seek the <u>**TRUTH**</u>.
<u>**SHARE**</u> *the truth.*

*Love Others (thy neighbor).*

*Love your(thy)Self.*

**WE ARE ALL ONE.**

**DUH. WAKE UP.**

David Dorn was murdered in the St. Louis RIOTS of 2020.
He served the community for decades as a police officer.
SAY HIS NAME. SAY HIS NAME. SAY HIS NAME.

Why didn't you know his name?
Pray for his family.
Pray for his community.
Not all cops are bad.

Patrick Underwood was murdered in the Oakland RIOTS.
He was a black federal officer that did not deserve to die.
SAY HIS NAME. SAY HIS NAME. SAY HIS NAME.
Where was BLM when these innocent men were murdered?!
Pray for his family.
Not all who serve are bad.

Staggering numbers of
Black lives
White lives
Brown lives
Blue lives
CHILD LIVES
ALL lives –
have been violently attacked, and senselessly stolen.
The media have failed you,
your families,
and the public at large.
I extend gratitude to the White House for sharing your experiences. We are all with you in your grief.

Those who know, know.

PRAY for the

**CHILDREN**

who

**tragically** and **violently**

lost their

**precious lives**

in this

**senseless** violence.

**Pray** for their families.
**Pray** for peace.

**PROTECT CHILDREN.**

**NO EXCEPTIONS.**

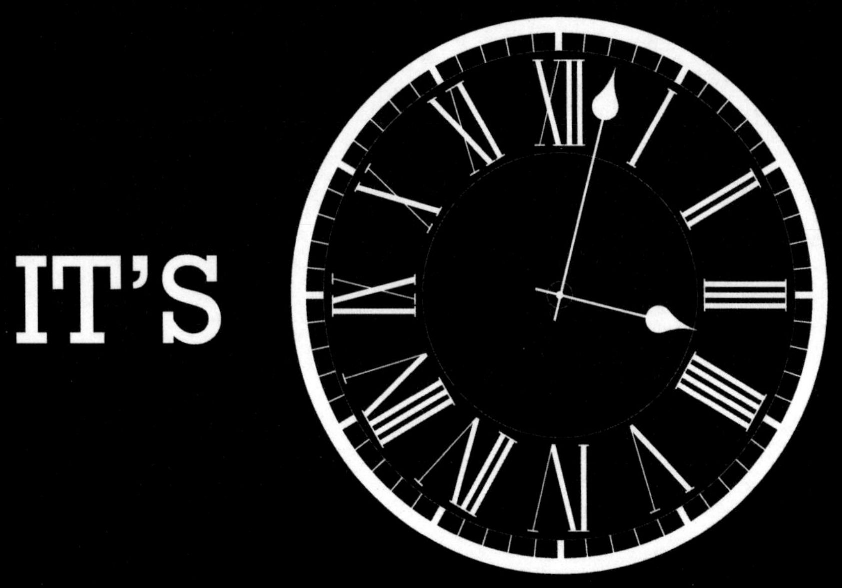


# TIME...

# WAKE

# UP

## MAKE NO MISTAKE:

If you were in support of the riots,

you supported the destruction of the Black community

and thus,

White supremacy.

Make peace with this today, and move forward in Solidarity.

Why were you in support of the riots at *any* time? Understand your own thinking.

**More Black children have been murdered in the US in the summer of 2020 than the Black criminals the media show being executed to push their sick narrative.**

**INNOCENT.**

**BLACK.**

**CHILDREN.**

**MURDERED.**

**BY THE DOZENS. By who?**

All because you think defunding the police is a cute and fun concept?!

Where are the riots for THEM?! Stop molly coddling and crying over criminals and start caring about CHILDREN.

The greatest injustice here is displaying the execution of Blacks for the entire world to see and further incite this disgusting politically-driven, media-fueled garbage attempt at a race war.

**This type of media is purposely used to further traumatize & enrage the public FAR past the incident which created the initial trauma.**

No trigger warning??
Widely available to all ages.

How about not viewing and SHARING snuff films?

Freaks.

SMH

# Trivia Time!!

Which group historically, in the US has used the

**TACTIC**

of burning down Black neighborhoods as to

**DESTROY**

Black economies and resources?

# BEING BLACK IS MY FAVORITE PASTTIME

Do you enjoy being your race?

Is it wrong to be proud of how you were born?

Does being proud of the way you were born make you better than anyone?

Worse?

If you don't like being the color that you are, why?

Who told you to think this way?

Is God/Source proud of the way you were born?

**Common racist misconception: Black people live in fear every day!**

**NEWS FLASH!!!!!!!!!**

# Every day in my skin is NOT Hell.

Do you ***really*** believe the great majority of Black people live in fear every single day?

If you do, you are stupid.

Stop perpetuating this false fakery.

# I LOVE BEING BLACK AS F*CK!!!

**BLACK**

BLACK

**BLACK**

**BLACK**

**BLACK**

**BLACK**

Stop referencing my **pain**.

Focus on my **power**.

**BREAKING NEWS:**

My ancestors would **NEVER** have destroyed their own neighborhoods.

And they suffered **FAR** worse atrocities.

Stop pushing the sympathy card by reciting to me my history and lived experience.

You don't know **shit**.

**Gentle Reminder:**

If you support(ed) the riots in any way, shape, or form, you can keep your donations and dust pans.

Too many of you stood idly by while you assumed Blacks were "rebelling" out of anger.

That is NO ALLY.
That is NOT SOLIDARITY.

Some of you *PARTICIPATED*.

**Seek forgiveness.**

If you shamed anyone for speaking out against the riots,

you were actively supporting White supremacist ideology.

# People of color do not need you to feel a certain way *on our behalf*.

**We got this.**

Feeling sorry for people isn't Solidarity.

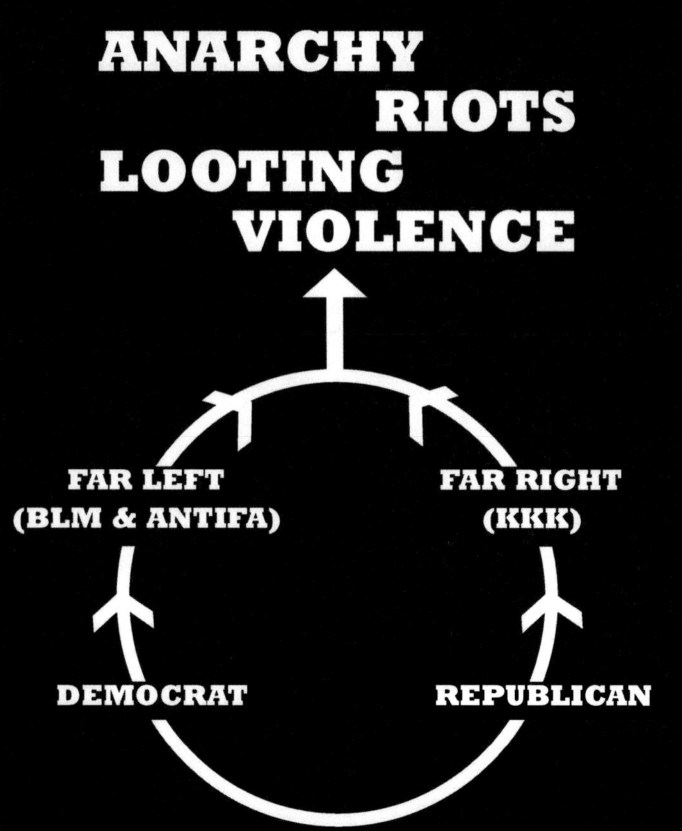


Don't swing so far **left**
that you

become the people

you claim to hate.

Someone who truly stands in Solidarity would never cheerlead for the destruction of those they claim to stand with.

**Scenario**:

A loved one is angry so they burn their house down.

Do you cheer them on for destroying themselves?

Is however they react to their anger okay just because they're upset? Would you not intervene?

Do you always make excuses for bad behavior?

**Remove thine thumb from thine bum. K thx.**

I have seen memes referring to Minneapolis as being so "gangster" they burned it down and cleaned it up the next day.

WTF kind of degenerate ass bullshit is that?!

The only time I have
EVER feared
White supremacy
was when I found out

(KL)Antifa was in town.

Outside of them, White supremacy is a non-issue in my life.

Your social media memes do not fully portray the Black experience.

Stop perpetuating stories you cannot confirm are true for all of us.

The narrative you have created is bullshit.

The assumption that Black people are violent, destructive, and ignorant enough to destroy their own neighborhoods, economies, and resources is inherently racist.

(Yes, the STUPID Black people took advantage of certain situations and the 400 pounders on megaphones stealing people's beers are Satanic paid Marxist puppets, but most of these BLM/Antifa snakes are White liberals)

Too many negative adjectives are being shared about the Black experience (living in fear, systemic racism, etc.)

Today, come up with 5-10 POSITIVE adjectives about Black people (strong, brave, innovative, etc.) rather than this downtrodden narrative you're so desperate to perpetuate.

Now do that for every race including your own.

Do any of these adjectives apply to multiple races?

Are these adjectives truer  or less true than the negative associations?

Which narrative perpetuates Solidarity?

Black Civil Rights monuments and memorials being burned and desecrated keeps me up at night.

It is sick that we have had to witness this in our lifetime.

Did they even cross your mind?

Why were they defaced?

Or were you too furiously concerned with the way Trump chose to care about them?

Remember St. John's Church

Remember the Lincoln Memorial

Remember the 54th Massachusetts Regime Memorial

And MANY more including abolitionists.

If you supported or encouraged Black people committing violent crimes during the riots considering this ever-important narrative of "Black genocide by police", you support White supremacist ideology. Except worse.

Black people do not believe destroying statues or removing Aunt Jemima from a syrup bottle combats racism.

We ***all*** loved Uncle Ben, Aunt Jemima, and The Land O' Lakes girl.

These are Black & Brown faces that had a noteworthy place in the homes of Americans of ALL colors.

Call me crazy, but that seems ***more*** racist to remove them to me...

Whites are killed by police too,
more often than Blacks.

Do those families feel no fear?

It is your job to STAND with us, not KNEEL before us.

These are humiliating practices.

Never put your lips one someone's dirty ass shoes.

We are not vengeful.

It is not useful to inflict on our former oppressors what they inflicted on us.

Violence does not solve violence.

We are past that.

KNEEL ONLY BEFORE GOD.

Donald Trump has implemented unprecedented legislation for the advancement of Black Americans economically.

What have you done to serve the Black community?

(Sweeping up riots and handing out money to terrorist organizations doesn't count, FYI.)

Fatherless homes and broken families are one of, it not **THE** biggest problems Blacks face.

Which group states on their website that one of their goals is dismantling the nuclear family?

(and then deleted it when it got attention)

What government policies encourage fatherless homes in the Black community?

Have these policies been abolished?

Who created these policies?

If you think all cops are bad…

You are stupid.

If all cops are bad,

are Black cops bad too?

…Even the ones who tirelessly serve the Black community? Let's use logic here kids…

**Antifa is worse than the KKK.**

They coax Black people into destroying their own communities after pretending to care for them.

Thus, putting Blacks at risk for the police brutality they say runs so rampant.

At least the KKK did it all themselves

Destruction of property **IS**
violence.

It **is** violence against the
economy,
resources,
and livelihood
of a neighborhood
and its residents.

Will you teach your children that
destroying their communities is
okay as long as you're mad?

**President Trump has done more for Black people and children than any other President.**

Those in our community who know the truth are grateful for his policies.

PRISON REFORM:
The First Step Act finally in action.

WELFARE:
President Trump's administration has millions of Black Americans OFF of government assistance.
(This is how wealth in the Black community is created.)

BLACK LIVES:
Donald Trump knows how many millions of unborn Black babies are killed in the womb.
He stands against this in heart, soul, and policy.
STOP KILLING BLACK BABIES.
PROTECT CHILDREN.

JOBS:
President Trump has created millions of jobs for Black Americans.
This is the lowest Black unemployment rate in 60 years.

EDUCATION:
President Trump has increased funding for HBCUs and extended their contracts.

After reading only a small list of what this administration has done to combat systemic racism at the federal level, can the hatred in your heart be lessened even slightly?
Why or why not?
If you still can't support these policies, what exactly the f*ck do you support?

If you think of a Black person when you hear the word "thug", you are racist.

■ ■ ■

There's a plethora of scary ass skinny ass cracky ass white meth heads out there a.k.a. Antifa.

These Antifa kids look like they have piss buckets next to their beds. Smh.

Please don’t overcompensate in any way because you are interacting with a person of color.

It’s more racist than just being yourself and allowing them to be themselves.

If you support Black-owned businesses & employment as an alleged "ally" yet supported the riots in any way,

your ideology is far more dangerous and sinister than that of White supremacy.

Putting a Black square on social media is not Solidarity.

It's laughable and a weak ass virtue signal at best but feels to me more like a slap in the face…

Your slacktivism is absolutely unbearable.

**Do Black people a favor:**

Check out some alternative news sources.

CNN clearly hates Black people.

Fuck Fox too.

The concept of White privilege perpetuates the concept of Black inferiority.

Black people do not want to be referred to as an acronym.

We didn't make them up as far as I know.

Don't be lazy.

POC

=

People of Color

=

Colored People….

Spare me with that diet woke BS.

"Free Services to POCs" is
**NOT**
**INCLUSIVE**
# LANGUAGE.

It is assumptive and promotes division & stereotypes based solely on skin color.

Claiming you are an ally requires *actual work*.

"Work" does not include mindlessly parroting the FAKE,

FALSE,

**FARCE**

that is the BLM admitted Marxists & the Antifa anarchists.

***White person claims to be an ally ***

Attacks Black conservatives online.

Demands they provide them with sources for their information rather than doing their own research

Refuses to do their own research

Rinse. Repeat.

***smfh***

The line of the times:

"I'm listening. I'm learning".
So then isn't it YOUR job to do research from ALL sides of an issue?
What are some ways you can seek out the other side of an(y) issue?

Attacking conservative Blacks online is *nonsensical*.

Give all perspectives fair consideration.

**Cuz, you know—**
**LeArNDing.**

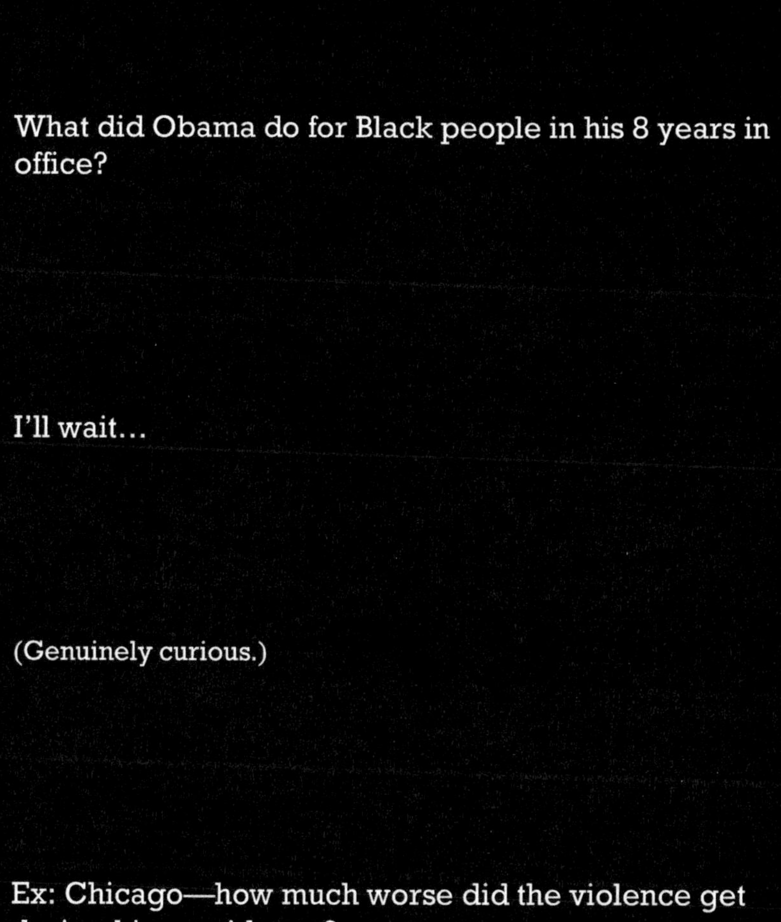

What did Obama do for Black people in his 8 years in office?

I'll wait…

(Genuinely curious.)

Ex: Chicago—how much worse did the violence get during his presidency?

When people in masks tear through
my neighborhood ...

Burning
and looting...

I am **TRIGGERED**.

You should be too.

Traumatic AF.

Why should/would this be traumatic for
Blacks? Hmm...

It's more damaging to ***say***
you are an ally
and then not ***act*** as one.

It is **more sinister** than
White supremacist ideology.

Talking about how oppressed you AREN'T and how oppressed someone else IS is NOT Solidarity.

Telling me I'm oppressed isn't Solidarity. It merely perpetuates fear, racial divide, and a bullshitting ass narrative.

Black people are strong. Brave. Powerful. Free. Innovative. Creative. We all are.

And that's a FAR better story to tell.

Liberalism has changed over the last 10-15 years.

Feels more like rabid wolves than social justice warriors.

| **Democrats THEN** | **Democrats NOW** |
|---|---|
| • **Burned down historic churches** | • **Burned down historic churches** |
| • **Wore masks to hide their shame** | • **Wore masks to hide their shame** |
| • **Destroyed Black neighborhoods** | • **Destroyed Black neighborhoods** |

Oh wait, those two things are synonymous.

Black people

**LOVE**

Law and Order

in their

neighborhoods.

Who doesn't?

How TF is calling the police privileged?

SMH

The movement and the message are ***two different things.***

One only gives a damn when cops are involved.

The other believes ALL Black lives matter.

How many Blacks are killed by other Blacks in America each year?

Where is BLM for *THOSE* atrocities?

Why haven't they used their nearly billion dollars in donations to actually improve/save black lives?

Where the hell is all their money going?

How many police interactions occur

each day?

Each year?

How many unarmed Black men are murdered out of that number?

Do the math.

Is this ***REALLY GENOCIDE***?

Why does BLM want to dismantle the nuclear family?

Blacks were thriving when families were whole.

Breonna Taylor's boyfriend failed her one final and tragic time.
Where is the hatred and disgust for HIM?
**WHEN YOU SHOOT COPS, THEY SHOOT BACK.**
**He knew that.**
No man who thought PROTECTING BLACK WOMEN AND CHILDREN WAS HIS PRIMARY DUTY IN LIFE would have their beautiful Black woman participating in illegal activities and knowingly putting her in harm's way by firing at officers.

# TAKE ACTION

**So, what the hell am I supposed to do with this information?**

# DON'T

Be coaxed into participating in a politically-driven race war.

Start up a group of White people to learn about Black people. You'll be more successful in your learning if you have Black voices in these discussions. Shit gets weird when one race sits around discussing another race.

Assume Black people act a certain way.

Allow Black economies and resources to be destroyed

Put your life in danger for any reason. (I heard Whites were asked to stand on the front lines of potentially dangerous situations. Please don't be that stupid...)

Get so offended so easily.

Feel a certain (assumed) way on the behalf of any race.

Use negative adjectives and associate them with all Black people. Or White people. Or any people.

Randomly talk about race out of context. These discussions deserve spaces created with thought and care.

Be so desperate not to be racist that you act in ways that show racial bias.

Financially or morally support Marxist/Communist organizations like Antifa and BLM.

Be a fucking crybaby.

Victimize Black people. Or White people. Or any people.

Make excuses for garbage ass behavior.

Hate the color of your skin, regardless of its' color. Its sick to do this, especially to teach your children this trash.

Resist cognitive dissonance. LEAN into it. Learning cannot occur without it.

## DO

Question your own thinking.

when and how you are being indoctrinated.

Raise your kids well.

Be a good person. Treat others with kindness.

Listen to conservative Black voices.

Study history from a number of perspectives. Get the FULL picture.

Talk to Black people you know.

Stop watching the news so much, or seek alternative news sources.

Read the entire article, critically.

Acknowledge and honor the freedoms we have in the United States. Many people across the world face crippling oppression every day.

Support family-owned businesses regardless of color.

Use positive adjectives when discussing good Americans of every race.

Share the hell out of this book.

Allow your children to lead their own learning and understanding about race.

Know and believe that most people are good.

Degenerates are NOT the majority.

Know you are worthy enough to have an opinion about the society you live in, regardless of the skin color God lovingly gave you.

Share these thoughts and your ideas respectfully and without fear.

Stand up for what you believe in, but only after careful thought.

# *Final Thoughts*

Violence is not okay.

Vandalism is not okay.

White silence is not violence. That's stupid.

If you stand in the middle of a riot, bad things will likely happen to you.

God/Source is always working for your highest good.

Know history.

Never be silenced, no matter your skin color.

Antifa is not just an ideology. Real people died. Real livelihoods were destroyed.

Know where you stand.

Know your bias.

Know yourSelf.

We are all One.

No race war. Get closer together.

#WWG1WGA #SAVEOURCHILDREN
#UNITYFORAGREATERAMERICA #KAG